DRAWING WITH WORDS

A Studio Concept of Composition

Michael Fink

Illustrated by Mary Fitzgerald
Edited and with a Preface by Katherine Scheidler

Copyright © 1981 by

University Press of America,™ Inc.

4720 Boston Way
Lanham, MD 20706

3 Henrietta Street
London WC2E 8LU England

Library of Congress Cataloging in Publication Data

Fink, Michael, 1933-
   Drawing with words.

   1. English language—Rhetoric—Study and teaching.
2. Art—Study and teaching. I. Scheidler, Katherine.
II. Title.
PE1404.F5   808'402'07073   81-40709
ISBN 0-8191-2039-1   AACR2
ISBN 0-0-8191-1963-6 (pbk.)

DEDICATION

My career at the Rhode Island School of Design has been to incorporate liberal arts within what are called fine arts — to attempt to give a humanist dimension to the conception of art itself. Over two and a half decades I have tried to bring various humanist media and events — the history of cinema in relation to depression and war, the literature of minorities, ecology — to bear upon the responsibilities and terrain of the designer or artist.

But now I feel the other side of the coin: that the eye of the artist is intrinsically humanist, and that the public itself is ready to acknowledge that design belongs to all humankind and to the shape of all experience.

Therefore, my book is offered to all who care to consider that writing is a human design for looking both out into the world and inward to one's own authentic capacity to "see" in every sense of the word.

I believe that writing and drawing are similar kinds of reflective activities: they mean thinking in concrete and personal terms, locating an honest perspective on the world. The essay itself is the essence of the humanist quest, and this book guides us toward the tradition and the heart of the essay, which means sketch, which means involvement. Involvement with just that touch of detachment which aids good judgment.

This book contains twelve writing assignments based on the problems assigned in the art classes taught at Rhode Island School of Design. From my collection of outstanding essays written to the assignments, I have gleaned a few illustrative examples to clinch the point of the set task. I thank my students for building this book and its approach with me. The Afterword attempts to have the reader look at the experience of this approach to composition through the eyes and ears of the students themselves.

The reader of this text may consider that language is a deeply human medium for the intimate perception of the world and one's place within the world. It hopes to bring to the public an idea of composition that implies an eye for beauty and detail, a taste for freedom and authenticity, and a recognition of weight and responsibility.

Thus this book, a labor of love, is dedicated to my students and to my readers, hoping that they will enjoy it, use it, and learn from it.

Michael Fink
Providence, Rhode Island

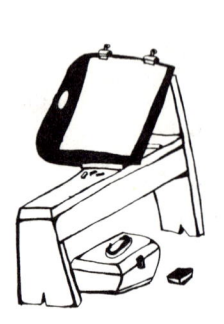

PREFACE

The work of writing is hard. What delight it is to read a paper when the work is original in thought and word, when it states a point and substantiates that point, when it shows that the writer cares about the subject. Then even correcting mechanical errors can be a joy for student and teacher. But how, we ask, can we ever get to that point?

Using Michael Fink's book to learn to write is like opening a window in a stuffy classroom on a spring day. Let's try it a new way, he says. Let's forget, for the moment, topic sentences, outlines, the reader-writer relationship, parallel construction and even fragments and run-ons. Let's forget writing assignments based on literature or even current events, where knowledge of the subject is required, where one can be wrong, where one may not care enough to want to write well. Let's draw pictures. And let's do it over and over again, creating different kinds of pictures, and let's talk about these pictures so we can all get better at it. The technique, he says, is born from the experience of seeing and writing, or it's not worth anything.

What is the value of this approach in a day when we all have to be more practical, when we have to worry about jobs, money, transcripts? What will describing a sidewalk, examining a face do for my career? the writer asks. Only this: drawing with words will give the writer a feeling for words, unity of impression, detail, ideas behind surfaces, originality of perspective. And through practice it will give one an ease in writing which is both a practical skill and a personally satisfying one.

Katherine Scheidler
Hope High School
Providence, Rhode Island

CONTENTS

Dedication   iii
Preface   v
Introduction   ix

I. Figure Model   1
Elizabeth
Untitled

II. The Object or The Still Life   3
Ping Pong Ball
Beach Glass
Kneaded Eraser

III. Two Dimensional Design (2 D)   7
Red Umbrella
String of Kites

IV. Space Paper: Three Dimensional Design (3 D)   9
Study
Harry's

V. Nature Sketch   13
Snail
Mouse
Dead Bird
Horse

VI. Action Sketch   17
Sidewalk
Bus Ride
Sled Ride

VII. Reflections on a Process   21
Drawing: Writing — The Creative Process
Breakfast

VIII. Portrait and Self Portrait   23
  Charlie
  Roger Hutton
  Chris

IX. Reflections on the Past: Drawing from Memory   29
  Pet Rabbit
  The Officer
  Grandmother

X. Drawing a Dilemma: Giving Form to Doubt and Fear   33
  Rat in the Storm
  Worse than Death
  Taste of Fear

XI. Sketch Pad: Building Perception from Observation   39
  Cold
  Nanny
  Three Veiled Nuns
  Chickens

XII. A Kind of Exam: The Final Project   45
  Moments Spent Alone

Afterword   49

INTRODUCTION

This suggested core of a course in composition meets few of the assumed urgencies of today's teaching: it has nothing to do with fast culture, speed reading, or quick and sure brush-ups in accepted correct usage of forms, spelling or punctuation, although these problems are indeed dealt with. It is a return to the origins of the language, not an advance toward a streamlined new approach. It is a belief that spelling is a way of looking at a word, enjoying its shape and inner story; punctuation is a rendering of tone, a pacing and spacing of thought. Rules need not be laid down, but can be discovered during or after working. This volume of essays suggests some possibilities of a personal approach to what to do with students in a writing and reading course, what to do with yourself in writing and in thought.

This approach has pleased some people who were intimidated by the technicalities of language teaching, impeded from entering the language at all. I am proudest of the fine pieces produced with pleasure by students who had always flunked or hated their English classes, hated language itself. It has also awakened writers who had had too easy successes and floated by without discovering the responsibilities and weights of their words and statements.

Problem I Figure Model

Sketch a figure model with words. Any person brought in from outside the studio-classroom can serve as a figure model. The emphasis in the writing must be on basic body shape, not on surface style or overt personality. Physical presence must be emphasized; rhetoric is based on weight, volume, scale, context, substance. Surprise and enthusiasm too must be generated from the task.

Imagine, for example: students arrive to class for a quiet roll-call. They do not notice a figure in ordinary robe-shaped dress until she easily slips out of it and onto a grey table placed at the center of the room, transforming classroom into studio. Once students accept that they are in the right room at the correct hour, they understand that they are to do a figure drawing in writing. They may be asked then to sketch the model right over their essays, and compare the two approaches.

Notice how in this brief essay the key words refer to the body reaching for the limits of the defining space. Concern lies with bulk, scale, center of gravity and linear curve.

Elizabeth

Elizabeth took advantage of the table's dimension. While the table was long, her body reached for its limits, conforming to the space defined by the table.

The pose concentrates the bulk of its mass near its exact geometric center. A curve climbs from her feet to a relative maximum at her hips. Here the weight of her form seems to express itself in her bent lower leg.

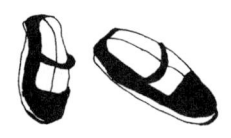

Although an outside model functions best, students can pose for each other, in a kind of guessing game. Or the instructor can make do alone. Note here how an honest, objective perception forces the sentences to jump and move about, to render the quality of a presence.

Untitled

The room was seemingly bare, only containing the essentials of a classroom — chairs with writing arms. The teacher entered. He was so unimpressive, ineffectual looking. His body, slight and thin, moved with a quick and nervous grace. He blinked, scratched his head, chewed hangnails, adjusted his glasses. Then he spoke. His voice boomed. How could such a strong voice come from such a tiny person? He commanded attention with his hands and arms waving and eyebrows shooting upward. His hands caught the air and moulded it, while his voice shaped it with words and pitch variations. The idea slowly took form from within and without. His speech too became a drawing, where, instead of a collection of marks, a collection of words formed the idea, playing with background objects, forming the space surrounding the idea.

Problem II The Object or The Still Life

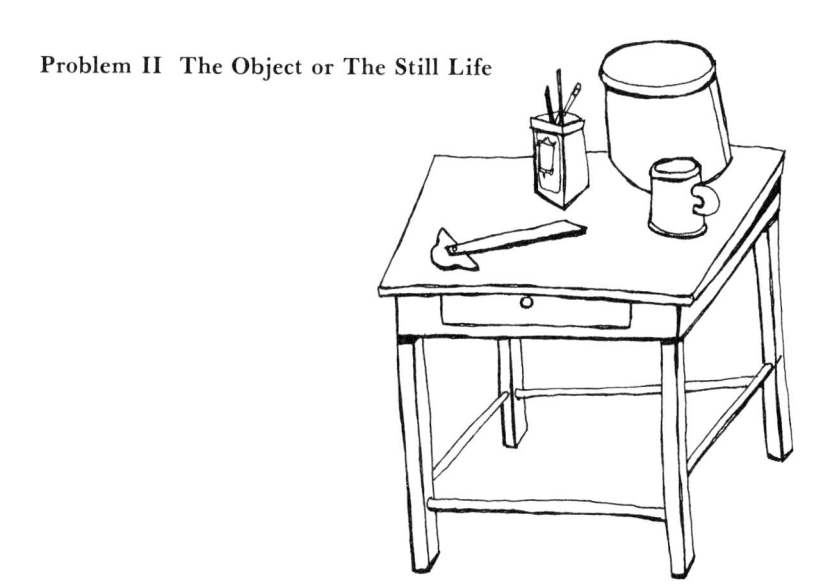

Choose some simple object, preferably common, humble, manageably small, and describe it without naming it. That is, recreate it for us in some organized way so that we will feel in the presence of the thing, satisfied, relaxed and content with our rediscovery of it.

A teacher may, for example, lug in a great load of fresh clay and without preparation invite the class to come to the barrel or box and take out a lump of this stuff, then spend a half-hour writing about it, not naming it. It's likely the student will make up a kind of riddle to indicate the **word** "clay." There may be references to the history and the future of the material, anecdotal and personified notions of the idea of clay, as if the **word** had been written on the board. We are not used to acknowledging the weight and feel of the earth in our hands.

In these student models, the best is the pingpong paper. It's no mystery, but without obvious references to its use, the form and vitality of the thing is given to us gracefully and aptly.

The kneaded eraser sketch uses analogies with imaginative success. That is, the way-out variety of images doesn't decorate or mislead, but conveys the texture and shifting shape of the material. In fact it describes the creative process, the self, the writer's self. Choice here is most important.

It's difficult to differentiate the particularities of an odd, small, obscure object. In "Beach Glass" the writer enjoys the problems comfortably and pleasantly.

All formal problems are given life and meaning via these object papers. That is, the object demands that the paper be organized, clear, unified, that the rules of writing come from things, from the unity of experience, not from artificial formulas.

Ping Pong Ball

KIP----------------------KIP----------------------KIP------KIP--------------KIP
---------------------------- K I P ---- K I P -- K I P - K I P K I P K IPKPKPKPKPKPKPPPPPPPP-----That's the sound it makes. It's small, small as a quarter; it's white, white as a sheet; it's spherical, spherical as the globe, and it's smooth, smooth as an egg shell.

As you observe it, it is hard not to notice how the light is reflected off its smooth surface in one small spot. On the opposite side there is a light grey crescent shape.

Turning it is no problem at all, for it weighs less than a fremit. While you turn it an orange spot hits your eye — the manufacturer's stamp, which is so small you can hardly read it. If you hold it up to the light, a dark ring forms around the inside of the translucent ball. Closer observation shows it's a seam, almost unnoticeable away from the light. This ugly, sneaky hidden seam is like a scar, a scar around this beautiful little creation.
KEE KEEEEE KREER KREEKK CRACKSNAP!!

Oh yes! It's very thin, but sturdy, to a certain point.

Beach Glass

It is amoebic in shape, something like an irregular half-moon. It is about half as long as your finger, bulging wider then narrowing smaller, hardly thicker than a piece of yarn. Its color is a frosty, pale lavender; behind it the fingers glow pink through its hazy inside. It curves smoothly beneath the touch, with the merest hint of roughness in its texture. Though it feels firm and solid to grasp it weighs almost nothing. On one rounded edge is a large, irregular chip, whose smooth, glassy surface contrasts with the cloudiness of the object, like a bite taken out of a gumdrop. On the other side are four faint, even lines, like ribs, in its surface. It is covered with thousands of tiny nicks, which catch the light and glint silver as you turn it over.

Kneaded Eraser

It is a small gray mass of material without a definite form, able to be stretched or squeezed into any shape. When pulled out like taffy it has the consistency of dust but the likeness of sinewy muscle. When clenched in the fist, it feels like hard putty, and looks like a smooth pebble on the beach. When wrapped around one's finger, it clasps gently like a baby, yet looks like ribbons on a May-pole. It combines with itself like bread dough, feels like gristle between the teeth, and all we do with it is pick up unwanted graphite from our paper.

In his office, Mike Fink with a background of 2-D assignments.

Problem III Two Dimensional Design (2D)

Write a description of a design you find on a two-dimensional surface — a large poster, a magazine ad, a commercial letter, a snapshot, cartoon, any kind of sheet of paper. Be careful not just to judge the message but to convey its form, its intent as revealed in the arrangement of its content. You may imply a judgment, but it must be contained within your perception of the size, texture, color, lines and proportion of the paper itself. It must suggest and show flatness.

In "Red Umbrella" the value of the assessment of the meaning of an ad lies in its close study of graphic design elements and specific layout. Notice the tracing of visual impact to the eye before the copy is narrated. Evidence and impression are compressed into interpretation.

Red Umbrella

The photograph is dark and blurry in the foreground, but a lighted band of white in the background draws your eye down the aisle between the desks to the rear of the classroom. There, a focused boy in a sweater is reading from a book on his desk. His knees are crossed, causing his pantleg to slide a foot above his ankle. He seems to be quite at ease, but wouldn't **anyone** feel relaxed and peaceful knowing they had a huge red umbrella looming directly above their head? The umbrella is superimposed on the black and white photograph, but it is carefully placed to emphasize that this one boy alone, and not the others in the room, is protected from all burden or worry.

After all, his father has taken out a Travelers Insurance Company Guaranteed College Fund. This, according to the caption below, means that if the boy gets grades that are good enough for college acceptance, he will have no worries for all his years in college. He will get four annual payments starting at the age of 18. Even if his father dies or is disabled for life, the boy still has no problems. Any discriminating father should feel it his duty to begin making the payments for his six-year-old college-bound son. For a slightly higher monthly payment, he can also take out health and life insurance on the same policy. This way the father gets to have a big red umbrella over his head, too, because he knows that all of his money won't go to waste if the boy doesn't live to finish high school.

Not all two-dimensional surfaces remain static. A major freshman 2-D project at our school is the design of a working kite. The studio then becomes a breezy seaside setting. From my office ceiling hangs a dusty collection of them, blocked from their freedom by a window that faces the bay. One student describes them in this context.

String of Kites

A string of kites, trapped from the wind, like frail fish dangling from the flourescent dock, the afternoon's catch hanging in the gallows of the office ceiling. A wisp of wind sifts in through the window, smelling ever so faintly of the distant sea, traces of far away childhood blowing in to release the quiet stillness, and sets their translucent bodies fluttering at the memories.

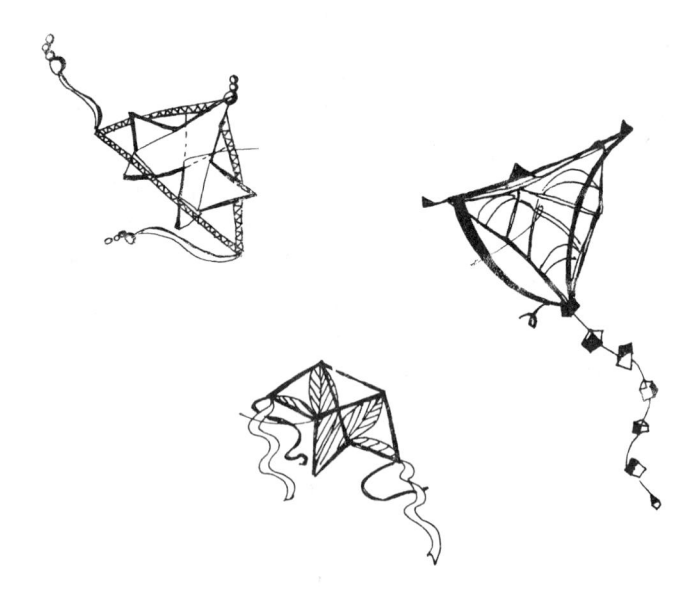

Problem IV

Space Paper: Three Dimensional Design (3D)

Recreate a room for us. But not your dorm room, not your bedroom or living room. If you must use your house, prefer the attic to the bedroom, the cellar to the parlor. If you use your dorm, the laundry room but not the lounge. If you go downtown, explore small stores or junkshops, not clothing departments or furniture salons. Because you'll merely list and judge, not create the total living scale and shape of your space. Grandparents' homes are better than friends' homes because they're cooler and more fixed. The problem is to create concrete and unified mood, not by naming or faking mood but by selecting those fixtures or sensually significant objects, sources of light and shadow, texture and thickness of wall, which together shape the roomness and tone of the enclosure you have carefully chosen.

A successful room paper is "Study," with its goldfish and its pine walls. Notice that the objects aren't just listed, they're set in place and interpreted with a driving motif. Each word helps to fortify the central concept. Here again, the room must take over and in a sense write itself. The paragraphs are judgeable by the standard set by the room. Not an intellectual room but a sensed space.

In "Harry's" look beneath the listings and you will note the composing of spaces and the organizing of activity into points of focus. The writer, from the inner city, writes from familiarity, not condescension. I especially like the bright yellow linoleum, because it performs the function of organizing chaos, and the use of the candy case to indicate the passing of time. The conclusion is not sentimental, and the pace is not desperate.

Study

The first thing you notice upon crossing the threshold of my study is the suddenly restful feeling that overcomes you almost at once. This atmosphere is revealed to be a synthesis of warm lights playing on waxed knotty pine walls, music undulating so softly as to barely make its presence felt, and tiny tropical fish finning silently and unquestioningly through their artificial world, transmitting a calming influence throughout the room.

Closing the door and crossing the carpeted floor on silent feet, you position yourself behind the low desk to get a better view of the surroundings. The heavy draw curtains which cover the windows seem strong enough to repel any alien disturbance. At the far end of the room are many shelves filled with magazines, notebooks, phonograph records and various other objects which your tired mind doesn't bother to identify. In the corner is a variety of camera equipment including a light stand and reflector, which resemble a gangly youth wearing a dunce cap. Your eyes are momentarily disturbed as they move across the light blue door and then relax again with the soft tones of pine paneling.

The next object to make itself seen is a television set, its electronic brain asleep and its huge eye staring blankly at the opposite wall into which is built a large suspended bookcase. The books in their colorful jackets are standing straight and tall, row on row, like a literary army, each waiting to reveal the secret wonders clutched between its covers. Here and there one of these soldiers of learning leans lazily on its neighbor, as though it has given up hope of being allowed to unfold its knowledge to some fortunate soul.

The eyes having now made a complete circuit of the room, your brain lumbers into motion to try to evaluate the information it has drawn through this pair of visual slaves. The entire effect is that of complete withdrawal from the outer world, a spell which can easily be broken by crossing again to the light blue door, turning the knob, and recrossing the threshold of my study.

Harry's

Harry's, as the neighborhood store is called, sits at the end of my street, surrounded by three-story tenement houses. Its front is dirty green and well worn by wind, sun, and rain. The front of the store serves as a support for those who are waiting for buses and as a substitute tree for the local dogs. A small door with a large, dirty window on each side adds to the ugliness of the building.

One's first impression on entering the store is confusion. This small shop contains enough merchandise to stock a supermarket. The variety of things sold ranges from hosiery and magazines to canned goods and semi-fresh vegetables. All items seem stocked with no thought to order, and only the experienced shopper can find what he wants immediately. The center of the floor is occupied by a pot-bellied wood stove, vegetable bins, jars of hard candy, a huge pickle jar, and a pile of five-pound potato sacks. Along one wall is a meat counter, along another an ice cream freezer, a coke machine and stacks of boxes.

Opposite the store's entrance is the main counter which runs the length of the store. Half the counter's space is taken up by an assortment of canned goods, hardware, and stacks of magazines and newspapers. The remaining space is occupied by a cash register, a greasy-fronted glass candy case, and a piece of bright yellow linoleum. This piece of linoleum acts as a center of interest in the confusion about it and is meant to act as such. At this spot money is exchanged between proprietor and customer.

The store's proprietor is Harry. This stout, gray-haired man looks the same now as when I used to press my face against his candy case. He still wears the same blue sweater and checkered shirt. A cigar stump is inevitably clamped at the side of his mouth. Harry is a businessman, a philosopher, and a gossip. While telling you who in the neighborhood died, he will talk you into buying some new product he has just obtained. When he is not complaining about organized religion, he is tearing down the state politicians. Harry has a unique viewpoint on many subjects, but few people agree with him.

The people who patronize Harry's are, for the most part, poor. Many have walked across the store's hardwood floors for years. When a new supermarket was built a few blocks away, Harry's customers still came at the regular rate. Harry's has become a neighborhood institution.

Today, the store still stands, only Harry is no longer there. Rising up behind the store is a wrecker's crane with its heavy steel ball demolishing the surrounding tenements. Soon Harry's, its customers, its outrageous prices, its outrageous bargains, and its familiarity will be gone.

Problem V Nature Sketch

Find some creature, some beastie, or bug, and write a paper conveying its quality of life to us. Don't take a dog, at least not your household pet, or a cute cat. In fact try to avoid the mammals — but only because they're too easy to personify, to give human character and Disney faces. They're too close to us — try to take on a mere worm, an earthworm, or reptile; turtles are good. If you want a bird, prefer the pigeon to the parakeet, the sparrow to the bright cardinal. You can ignore these warnings; they're made only to ward against the evasions of the picturesque, the anecdotal. Be sure really to encounter the creature, don't merely recall it, or make it up from pictures or an abstract idea. Don't kill it and describe its corpse — neither literally nor figuratively. Don't do a report on the beast, but try to render its movement, its pattern or mode of being. Remember too that you have one animal with you in a particular place, not a whole species. Avoid the general and be particular. Perhaps postpone naming the creature, so you won't rely on the public image but will recreate an image, organized and directed for us.

The snail paper that follows is good because the snail forces the writer to give us an immediate sense of scale and shape. She does this not with derivative measurements, inches, a delaying abstraction hard to visualize and dull to the senses — but she gives us the walnut. She works without constraint or affectation with comparisons, always to give us the snail in its snailness. The paper's small, and it's an early piece, but it moves like and with the snail.

The still life on the dead waxwing was written by a lover of living birds. But he brings the splendid light of his visual interest to bear also on an inert form, to which he lends movement and life.

Mouse paper has a good mouseness, too. It conveys the mouse's nervous wariness without just naming those traits; it shows them as it moves with the mouse. The mouse is not some idea of mouse, has no Mickey qualities, it's a lab mouse and remains one. Yet it interests us because some inner principle is worked out for us. Even its inky eyes shimmer with movement; nothing inert stops the mouse from frantic fervor.

Finally, the horse story, enthusiastic and spirited, remains responsible and unsentimental. The horse is there, the writer is there, and the whole encounter is objectified. Limitation of space for the creature intensifies our observation; a lesson for all rhetoric.

The problem in the creature papers is to accept the animal on its own terms, to render its way of carrying itself, not impose any artificial jargon onto it, scientific, technical, or sentimental. It implies your relationship to life itself, through another order of life.

Snail

The shape of its hard but thin black shell is fat and round, about the size of a walnut. Delicate white lines spiral to a short peak. From the mouth of the shell a greyish mass protrudes and spreads against the glass like a glob of melted wax. The head is a smaller shape — like a pea — with two tentacles extending out in curving, turning, rubber horns. The entire snail moves along the surface of the glass like an ice cube melting slowly downhill. As it moves, its mouth opens and shuts rhythmically like a beating heart against the glass.

Dead Bird

I was walking toward the college this morning, early, enjoying plowing through the blanket of leaves on the sidewalk. I was thinking that it gives one the same sensation as forking through a full plate of spaghetti.

I stopped walking abruptly as it occured to me that I had just seen something which was out of context on the sidewalk; something that didn't fit in with the leaves, pebbles, twigs, and scraps of paper. A neatly wrapped package that someone has just dropped has this quality, or a dollar bill.

I returned to the object that had struck my eye...

It is a dead bird. I crouch down over it and identify it as a cedar waxwing.

He is lying on his back, his head turned to one side. The head has the quality of a rich pen drawing: sharp, incised quickly, but deftly drawn. The beak sharp, finely shaped, the color of armor; the eye half closed but still moist, with a velvet, black stripe of mask across it. The forehead sweeps back from the beak over the eye into a refined crest. The head and neck merge smoothly and swell into the shoulders.

His body is like a passage in a Turner watercolor, from the warm coffee-brown head and chest to the delicate faded yellow of the stomach to the cream white at the base of the tail. His tail is solid grey, while the tip of it looks as if it had been dipped in pure cadmium yellow paint. Blue-grey wings are held formally along his sides, and the finely armored feet are curled, as if each was holding a small jewel.

Here was the waxwing, with all the elegance of a painting by Vermeer, without a feather out of place — perfect — his head turned sideways as if he himself had turned it that way as he died. He had the quality of a prince or an archbishop.

Later that day a girl told me that there is a disease that goes around among the birds at this time of year, that hits them quite suddenly with a shivering spell, and then they die. Maybe that's why he died, though I don't really know.

Mouse

He never stops moving; when he isn't scuttling around meekly from one corner of the small wire cage to the other, he sits quivering in a nervous little ball. Every hair of his coat seems to vibrate, especially his whiskers, which he constantly works back and forth timidly, much as a bat uses his radar or a blind man his cane. Almost lost in the shapeless blob of his fur are four brightly pink, delicately formed feet; each flawless toe is covered by a harmless silken claw. As he nervously nibbles his food, he handles it dextrously with his miniature hands. His pink wormlike tail seems to have a life of its own, it weaves along like a snake, forming its own patterns as it trails behind him. Most fascinating to examine are his transparent tissue paper ears, which are so micro-thin that each vein can be easily distinguished. His tiny black eyes, shimmering like beads of India ink, are constantly darting in all directions about him, watching for the slightest sign of danger that will send him darting to the safety of his nest.

Horse

Today I saw a horse, a horse whose head loomed way above mine as he slowly turned it to look at me. His eyes were a dark chocolate brown, glowing with flames of light between the shadows of his lashes, deep set in the hollows of his fine V-shaped face. His neck muscles stretched out as he lowered his softly breathing nostrils to sniff the sleeve of my coat. Slowly, rhythmically, his nostrils billowed out disclosing the vital red of the inside, just as a bellows, when pumped, fans a slow red glow among the black coals. And then he sneezed, his very own horse sneeze, and I laughed to see the golden grains of hay-dust hop up and catch the light and then settle on his coat. His coat was of the same color, smooth, golden hair tapering toward his tail. I reached up and patted his neck. His skin was like velvet and as I ran my hand over a vein, I could feel it throbbing with life. Then he turned his head from me and munched again on the hay.

In delight, I turned to the stable girl.

"What a horse!"

"Yeah," she replied, "but his front legs are gone, and he's going to the glue factory next week."

I turned again to the horse and looked down at his front legs. Finely shaped, they were a deepening golden brown blending into the black of the hoofs. The legs were placed close together, stiff and straight. But all at once one bent out like a rubber band, and the horse was left balancing his weight on one leg.

Problem VI The Action Sketch

Take a walk and describe the experience. But don't just list the places you go to and create an anecdote. Keep the walk alive, and convey the kind of impression walking creates. Or, take some kind of ride, a bike ride or a bus ride. Move with the train, canoe, plane, sled — and render the quality of movement, the separate and total kind of being and feeling you have in motion through space. Be a movie camera.

In the sidewalk paper the sidewalk itself is given a legitimate kind of life. Though the enterprise is personified, there **is** a real sidewalk moving with the wanderer. Our satisfaction in these motion papers depends on the completeness, consistency, authenticity of the writing. I think the most complete and consistent job is in the bus ride. The girl who wrote it was the tiniest, most elfin wee young lady. Keep that in mind as you consider the paper and its authenticity will be further felt.

This is really a study of the **verb**, but movement must be conveyed in the full texture of its immediacy. "Sled Ride," for example, takes us along on the ride.

Sidewalk

Here I stand, alone and friendless, not knowing where I am or where to go. Feeling conspicuous, I begin to walk. My random footsteps echo off the obscure and unfamiliar buildings which rise up out of my world. My only companion is a creature which stretches before me, section upon section, like a curious reptile wriggling around every corner and sliding silently down every street and into every alley, leading me on, daring me to follow, knowing only too well that I have no other choice.

Rounding a corner I meet an ageless friend, but even his friendliness disappears as he nips at my face and hands, tears at my clothing and then rushes off down the street. Clutching my coat more tightly around me I realize how quiet it is down here while so much is going on right above my head. Held in the grasp of an infinite chain of messengers, an unending flow of voices, music, cold, warmth and light travels through seemingly lifeless wires. Friendly voices, soft music and warmth are only a few feet away, while in the cold dark night I hurry along. Hurrying only because it is cold and my way is the way of chance. To the onlooker I seem to be going somewhere, but in reality I am going nowhere. Up one street and down the next, across a black river of pavement and then back to my ever searching companion. I do not know what he is looking for, up and down the lonely streets, but I think I will help him look.

Bus Ride

Making one's way from the fare box to the back of the vehicle is a kind of battle — short but strangely exhausting. The floor beneath is an uncertainty. It rocks and rumbles with a steadiness that makes progress down the aisle a bounding and rebounding, tennis ball style, off the bodies that form walls on either side. The path keeps changing from uphill to downhill, so that it is either labored climbing, pulling one's feet and pushing one's body against something invisible, or uncontrolled trotting that bounces the body's weight with increasing momentum.

Occasionally the floor jumps and disappears momentarily, and my body flies until my outstretched hand catches a pole. Then I am revolving on an axis — feet feel glued to the floor and the torso's weight swings in rhythmic arcs. Gradually the body becomes attuned to the stationary rocking. Muscles become fixedly tense to maintain balance, innards jog quietly, and skin ceases to notice the continual bumping against other bodies.

The plastic cavity of the seat is a couple of sizes too big — its curves are wide enough to make it feel uncomfortably unfilled. My derriere jumps and slides quietly in the hollowness of the curve during the distance of each block. At stops the seat would spill me if I didn't hold on.

It is a sort of tubular, turquoise and silver theatre. Brick walls, trees, store windows fly by like frames of movie film in the row of windows across the aisle. Viewed from this stage, the street below is unreal — cars are only shiny tops and squashed people look up.

Rumbles beneath the vibrating floor are steady, but open into the belches and muted screams each time the rocking swings harder and then lurches to a stop. The exit blinks open and exhales strangely; then becomes part of the wall again when it blinks closed.

It is an effort to rise and start walking again, like trying to break out of a magnetic field or to un-nail my feet from the floor. But once freed, movement forward is uncontrolled. Progress to the exit is a series of jerking lunges, descent into the pit by the door is almost involuntary, and emergence onto the street is more like being flung out. Then oddly, immediately, all impressions of the ride leave the mind, and only breathlessness and a strange fatigue remain to be savored in this newly still and solid environment.

Sled Ride

The wind and wet filtered coldness through my heavy sweater and jeans, while my boots crunched in the new wet snow. I grabbed the pull rope lying in the snowbank near me and yanked. Chunks of snow flew back and the dull silver and scraped wood of my sled jumped up on the edges of the runners. I flopped it down next to me and dragged it out into the street. The snow plow had gone by, leaving a thin slick coat of snow over the rough, gravel street. The sled glided instinctively forward as it touched the slippery path. I held it back till I could pull my cap tight over my senseless ears. Then I dropped my knee onto the hard wood and my furry hands clutched the steering bar. My stomach thudded onto the flatness and with the light whisper of the runners I moved past the mailbox and snow banks. A biting breeze hit my nostrils and flickered my eyelids. With a swoosh I missed the banks of the first corner and flew crookedly into the middle of the street. I sailed airily over a lump and down, down, down until the road ahead was flat. Slowly the wind drew away from my face and the swishing sound under me became a crunch. I still slid as determinedly as the drop on a melting icicle. Then, with a tight lurch, the ride was over.

Problem VII Reflections on a Process

Choose some simple activity, focus upon and carefully review the process, accentuating the sensual details. Quite naturally your sense of time will tend to slow down, so be careful not to let ludicrous and grotesque effects overwhelm your piece. It should be bright and spirited, and a little surprising. Don't be sensational or adventurous. Let the choice be natural and focused.

This assignment tends toward artificiality, and the best result was the study of drawing. It is swift, sure, and vital. The process of drawing is analogous to the act of composition: the paper reveals how drawing and writing take form from the nature of the experience.

One year a student described in detail tying her shoelaces in the morning — a process that said, Saddle me up for the day. Another, by coincidence, analyzed untying her boots at day's end. There is a strange satisfaction in focusing tightly, like a camera, onto an ordinary routine until it suggests character. In "Breakfast" the writer reveals through cereal clattering into a bowl his hesitant, nervous sensitivity.

Drawing : Writing — The Creative Process

When the drawing begins, I am caught up in the mad sweep of the charcoal pencil which moves of its own accord. It leaves me behind, helpless, hoping for something to emerge from the slashing lines. I am limited to the pencil's motion and quick looks at the model who sits waiting for the moment when the pose will crumble around her as she stirs and stretches her arms. I race to beat that moment, my thoughts gradually catching up with the pencil, curbing its frantic movements; astonished, I find a figure emerging before me on the paper.

Breakfast

As the small, round donut shaped biscuits tumble from the box into the bowl, they make a light rattling clatter that sounds like rain on a window. They are leveled off by my laying my hand over them, crushing them down somewhat. Now that they are level, the milk is poured in, raising and disrupting everything, as the cereal floats to the top. As the milk runs in, it all looks like a growing mass trying to push itself over the edges, but as it tries to sneak over I rap it with my spoon and sink it into the milk. After I've dunked them enough in this manner, they begin to soak up some milk and stay at one level. To put sugar on them, instead of sprinkling it on, I just dump it in one spot, where it sinks to the bottom. I distribute the sugar by mixing the whole conglomeration in a way which disturbs the floating mass as little as possible. This is done by agitating the spoon with a fast, short movement parallel to the bottom, and in the milk below the floating cereal.

At breakfast I always eat alone, and my posture is very bad. I sit in a slouched position with both elbows on the table and the left hand holding up my head. This, however, is not a bad position because the spoon does not have far to travel in going from bowl to mouth. The spoon never seems to hold enough to make one trip worth its while, so it takes two or three to make a mouthful of them. At first they make a crunching sound as they are chewed but that sound soon disappears, and they become a mushy ooze which slides between the teeth. At this rate they are soon gone except for a few left in the last spoonful of sugary milk.

Problem VIII Portrait and Self-Portrait

Write a character sketch, but not of someone you know well or care about deeply. Choose someone you've observed over a length of time without being fully aware of it, and know only in a limited and routine manner: the postman you hardly speak to, a waitress at a crowded cafe whom you merely watch, a janitor or bank teller. Avoid "The Most Unforgettable Character I've Ever Known," avoid the Bar Mitzvah address to your parents or the prize-winning tearjerker. What we're interested in of course is the keenness of your observation of gesture and detail, your establishment of some suggestion of personality, not an overt and overstated cliche. Self-portrait can become self-revelation or self-mockery: overweights and anorexics literally turn attitudes into flesh.

The paper on Charlie the model shows a good, clear, apt choice of subject. Through action, form and phrases Charlie comes to life for us.

Another fine example of the character sketch is the Roger Hutton paper. Bear with the slow pace for the sake of the great interest and rich involvement of the writer. The sketch uses a comic kind of underlined repetition and heavy triumph, weakness becoming tyrannic strength. Roger cannot, will not, accept conformist high school values, violates every high school code, while our author clearly shows his own self-righteous condescension. Roger is a comic character, he persists in being himself, and we have to celebrate this. Yet his pain is real, and this gives a responsible weight to the whole drama.

In the sketch of Chris, though the choice is of a roommate, about whom we often have strong overt attitudes, this writer keeps elegantly to the physical. This constitutes a victory over easy expository habits.

We should feel the presence of the person taking over the paper, shaping it there for us. The conclusion should reveal the surprise of insight, not a mere flat emphasis. The self-portrait must accentuate the physique, the destiny of flesh, not "spirit." Flesh **is** spirit.

Charlie

Big Charlie is a sort of imposing figure but his face is that of a little boy. You feel that he does not have a great amount of intelligence, and think he needs to know little to model for classes.

To watch him get ready to take a pose you tend to think him amusing as he carefully arranges his sponges and bamboo sticks, often stepping back to peer at them and scuttling up to rearrange one a half-inch and looking at them again. Finally he ceremoniously removes his robe and bit by bit he takes on a pose he will hold for practically the whole period.

After twenty minutes everyone takes a break. Charlie puts on his robe and wanders into the hallway where the students talk and smoke. He looks lost as do all the models when they are among the students. I say hello and we are soon talking about many things, especially modeling. I become aware that this is a person who is extremely happy in his chosen profession and proud of his achievements, which grow all the time, even to include a contract with a college in New York and a few bit parts in films. He knows more about his work, I realize, than I know about my chosen profession or will know for a while yet.

We talk about other things, his wife, his home, and the separation he has suffered. I don't mind listening and Charlie really wants to talk to someone. He stands like a high school kid, a little bashful in spite of his tall figure and powerful, though a little flabby, frame.

The break is over and students are coming in. With a lopsided grin Charlie shows his gratitude.

"Thank you for...being you," he says to me, and then returns to his pose.

Roger Hutton

When Roger Hutton was nine years old, his mother deserted him and his father: Roger claims she did this "because I was so ugly she couldn't stand me." Two years ago, when Roger was eighteen, his **stepmother** threw him out of the house: he claims she did this "because I was so ugly she couldn't stand me."

Thrown out by his stepmother, Roger was forced to go on relief to finish high school. From the $15.00 a week he received from welfare, he had to pay $7.00 rent for a tiny room in an ancient rooming house which has since been condemned.

Roger complained that he was ugly. This was true, to a point. He wore thick glasses and was bug-eyed. His chin receded sharply, he had bad acne, and he greased his hair against his head. His teeth were yellow and rotted. But Roger did nothing to aid his appearance. First of all, he hardly ever washed either his person or his clothes. Instead he would douse himself with cheap perfume, hoping to cover his odor. But the perfume combined with his sweat to form a third and most obnoxious scent. Roger never brushed his teeth or went to a dentist, and so his breath was foul. His complexion would have been better had he washed it or regulated his diet. Once, when Roger complained to me that no one could stand him, I suggested that he might be more likeable if he washed himself, his clothes and his teeth. He replied that he didn't wash because the drunks in his roominghouse were always in the bathroom and they laughed at him; he couldn't afford to wash his clothes; and, as for his breath and acne, since he was so ugly anyway, why should he even try? When I said this wasn't completely true, Roger shoved his face close to me, and, with foul breath, said, "Oh yeah? How would **you** LIKE TO HAVE **THIS FACE**?"

Roger was prone to throwing temper tantrums. Once in art class he dropped a pile of papers, which flew all over the floor. Seeing this, he jumped up and down on them, and then sat down and cried...

When I was a junior, I took part in a musical at school, which Roger was also in. There were over a hundred persons in the cast. More than sixty were girls. Well, the musical took place about a week before the junior prom, and Roger was desperate. Beginning with the beautiful starlet (he always believed in aiming high) and working his way down, Roger asked EVERY SINGLE GIRL in the musical to the prom. Needless to say, all refused him, the first because they loathed him, and the few who might have accepted because they could not tolerate being ROGER'S fiftieth choice. So on closing night, Roger threw a gigantic crying fit, and threatened to quit the musical "BECAUSE NO ONE LOVED HIM." It took a whole regiment of people close to an hour to comfort him enough so that he would consent to act his three lines.

Roger was always asking for criticisms of his paintings, which were atrociously bad. If the person asked did not like them, Roger was certain to abuse him. Once he showed me a woodcut he had done, one of his better pieces. It was the figure of a woman nailed to a crucifix. When he asked me my opinion, I declined to evaluate it but said that it must be his mother, whom he hated. My art teacher thought it represented women in general. Roger later showed the piece to his state-paid psychiatrist, who concurred with me that it was his mother. When Roger told me I must be clairvoyant, I assured him it was a matter of elementary psychology.

At the time, I was in the midst of a socialist crusade, and self-righteously decided to make myself Roger's friend and protector. For a time I brought him around with me and tried to get him to stand on his own. But Roger was a disappointment, and I soon discovered that there were things I could not do when I was with Roger.

For instance, I could not talk to girls with him around. I remember one incident when I was talking to a girl I knew and he was just standing there. Suddenly he said, "I'll see you," in his most dejected voice, and walked away stiffly — when Roger was upset, he walked like a robot, or Frankenstein. I went after him, and catching up, asked him what the matter was. He spat angrily, "EVERYONE HAS A GIRL EXCEPT ME — NO ONE WANTS ME..."

I often had to protect the girls I knew from Roger, lest they become too compassionate. Roger's favorite scheme was to demean himself before a girl, at which point she would assure him he was a "worthwhile individual." Then Roger would be all over her; often she would be too embarrassed to reject his advances.

The last time I brought Roger with me was to a dance on a Saturday night last spring — he had asked me several times to take him, and I finally gave in. After getting to the dance, Roger came over to me and told me, stiffly, that he didn't fit in here, that all these popular and successful kids couldn't possibly stand him. I was impatient and found an excuse to duck away. I spoke to him around an hour later, and he complained that no girls would dance with him — this was true, for the girls I knew did not wish to have Roger crushing them against him and snatching at them, something which he would do to any girl who would dance more than once with him. Later, Roger disappeared, and I secretly hoped he had gone home. But when I was driving away, I saw a figure in the moonlight backed up against a tree as if facing a firing squad. Knowing who it must be, I pulled up, rolled down the window and said, "O.K., Roger, get in." Roger approached the car with his robot walk and got in. As I was driving away, he held his stomach and began to groan — I must mention here that when Roger wanted pity, he would often have sudden inexplicable "pains." These pains must have gotten worse as I drove, for he was soon doubled up on the seat. I was in no mood to take it, and therefore said not a word. When I got to his house I asked him what the matter was, and he said "his stomach hurt." So I just told him he should go to bed, and said goodnight.

After that our relationship cooled. Soon Roger was busy making new friends to lean on. He is still back in Newport; I saw him when I went home several weeks ago. Apparently he had enlisted in the Air Force, but they refused for some reason to take him, so he got a job in one of the local stores and lives as always.

Chris

Chris shambles into the tiny room and gently eases his gargantuan form onto the wooden bed. He takes off the hiking boots that look like blackened loaves of pumpernickel bread. He sets them carefully beside the dangling control box of his pale electric blanket. His shoulders jerk in two quick nervous movements that dissipate into almost imperceptible shivers coursing down his lengthy frame.

His hands — they are great warm things — lie entangled in his lap. He flexes them together then thrusts his head against the wall. He nods his head and is ready to be sketched.

Chris's face is vaguely equine. There are the same broad nostrils on either side of a wide bone bridge. But his eyes are, perhaps, more like those of a goat than of a horse because the pupils are nearly almond-shaped. They lie on a flat hazel iris as the kind of minor deformity that makes people exotically attractive.

Unlike horse or goat, this man has full human lips. The bottom lip is the fullest, as is not unusual in males. Yet Chris's lips are not at all sensual — they are actually a little swollen. This has a tendency to blur the fine lines that delineate his mouth. Even so, there is a strong horizontal movement in his mouth that nicely repeats the breadth of his nostrils and the span of his forehead.

Two very dense eyebrows meet immediately above the eyes. They add a saturnine appearance that is almost a little garish on young faces. They bring the eyes racing down the nose so as to make Chris appear nearly cross-eyed. As a result, Chris' glances often seem out of focus. This myopia adds to the sense of introspection I often receive from Chris.

After some pop hero, my roommate has let his hair grow to below his shoulders. It hangs not sculpturally but two-dimensionally — almost as if it were a paper cut-out rather than a palpable form. The hair is a dull brass that casts subtle olive shadows on the temples.

Chris has fallen asleep. His frame appears structureless — almost nonexistent. His face is slumped on a broad shoulder that yields with a fleshy indentation. His cheek, because of the acuteness of the angle, hangs away from the face. For a moment the face is bloated and grotesque. But now a deep sleep comes, and somehow the features take on some of the dignity they hold in thinking hours. Perhaps he is dreaming.

At Daddy's office, Emily contemplates the past.

Problem IX Reflections on the Past: Drawing from Memory

Write a memory paper. Don't pick a recent memory, a prom or the day you were accepted to school. Find an early memory, preferably neither extremely happy nor unhappy. Render the process of memory. It's a memory paper: memory distorts and transforms. Let this happen. Let memory shape you a paper. In the stage notes to his **Glass Menagerie**, Tennessee Williams said these things about memory:

> Memory omits some details; others are exaggerated, according to the emotional value of the articles it touches, for memory is seated predominantly in the heart.

Thus the logic of this paper is just the logic of full and clear expression. Has memory in fact been revealed, or just a trite anecdote narrated? We want to see time, so don't pretend you're still a child, but remember as you are what you were, did, felt then, long ago. What has happened since?

Despite its shocking content, the rabbit sketch is one of the most perfect successes with the project, because it strongly shows how memory can color, or silence, or focus, or fix the mind. The description of the chair is absolutely necessary to convey the experience of the child and of the writer grown up. It doesn't create cheap and superficial suspense, but renders mysteries of consciousness and unconsciousness.

In the memoirs "Officer" and "Grandmother" the conjunction of sugar cubes with guns; the leap from Bonny, a sweetheart, to bunny, a toy, give a species of humor, grim or nostalgic as the case may be. They show how memory can be rendered directly, not through mere commentary.

Pet Rabbit

I was bowing forward and leaning backward so far that the stopping chocks of the old rocking chair jolted my neck against the wood with each rebound. I liked making the chair go as fast as it could. It was like being pushed way up in a swing. My arms stretched out and up from my elbows so I could get a good grip on the chair arms. The rocker was brown with a dark yellowish grain. Its finish was either cheap shellac or Butcher's wax, because when I scratched my hand across it, something brown and gummy got under my fingernails, leaving scrapes in the wood. When I curved my neck way over backward, I could see the square top of the back. On both sides the largest dowels ended in spheres and acorn shapes. There was a curved board with carvings on it, and near my head were rows of discs like the colored beads on playpens, except that these wouldn't move on the wire.

My mother stood in her usual position by the sink in front of the two windows with all the little ornaments and frilly curtains. She was drying dishes with a bright red cloth. I think she was always washing dishes, and I was always watching from my rocker by the hot water heater. I started rocking more slowly as I twisted my head around to find the bunny. We had a white baby rabbit that hopped around the kitchen — we treated it like most people treat their cat. I think it had a house in the back yard, too. I couldn't see him by the water heater or by my mother or anywhere.

"Mamma,...."

"Yes," she said, turning around to face me. I stopped rocking.

"...where is my bunny-rabbit?"

She took a scanty glance around the room and then stared at the floor behind me. I climbed around backwards without getting off the padded seat to see what she was looking at. Under and part way around one of the wooden rockers was what looked like some white fur gloves splashed with ketchup. I didn't know what it was for sure, but I knew that I must have been rocking on it. My mother rushed over to me with the dish cloth and started saying things. I think it was about how I rock too hard anyway and look at the poor, poor bunny, and I don't remember any more.

Officer

My memories start from the time I was three years old, and from the beginning they have always been connected with war. We lived outside the town in a suburb of Bucharest where it was much safer and easier to find food. I was forbidden to say that I was a Jew, and I enjoyed this conspiracy as I lacked the fear of things I didn't understand. I lived in a happy, childish dream where my toys were bullets and fragments of bombs and my heroes were soldiers.

I can remember especially a handsome officer who always stopped at my gate to play with me. It was a good friendship in spite of the difficulty of languages. He didn't know that I was a Jew, and I didn't understand that as a German he was my enemy. I was always firing at him with an imaginary gun, and he used to turn his eyes in their sockets and pretend to be dying.

Then one day the tanks came. For several days fighting took place around my house and we hid in the basement. When the battle was over and our neighborhood was safe again, we went up and out to see what had happened. I saw my handsome officer lying dead in the street. It took me a long while to understand that this was not a part of a game.

A short time after this incident, the Russians came into the city, and I clearly remember being perched on my father's shoulders to watch the parade. They passed in cars, trucks, tanks, and on foot. The crowd around us cheered and waved red flags. But what I remember more clearly than anything was that soldiers threw cubes of sugar to the boys who ran after the trucks. I wanted also to have one of their marvelous white pieces of sugar, but I was too proud or too ashamed to run after the trucks and collect the sugar from the dust.

Grandmother

My grandmother was a gentle faced, plump Russian. I remember staying with her when I was three years old. We would take the trolley-car downtown. On the way back home, she held my hand as I walked along the top of my favorite white, octagonal tile wall, and we would giggle and joke.

She would make me cabbage borscht and sour cream cookies; once she even let me make my own soup of water and barley, which I fed to her and to my stuffed red monkey. She made me nightgowns and let me feed the guppies in the bowl on a tall metal stand. I loved to hear over and over how she and her sisters picked mushrooms and berries in the woods when she was a girl in Russia, and she would tell me about "Babushka" and about the "Bonny-Rabbit" and the wolf.

I would sit shoulder deep in water in the enormous tub as she gave me a bath and washed my hair. I hated when all the warm water came pouring down my face and, worst of all, when she cracked a raw egg into my hair because, she said, it was good for it.

She would sing Russian folk songs and "My Bonny lies over the ocean." I thought it was about a rabbit, my green stuffed, and I couldn't stand the thought of it being far away across the ocean.

She put me to bed on the davenport. I remember sitting on the bed and watching her undress, or dress, unlacing and unstrapping her huge pink corset, her round figure dimly silhouetted against the window.

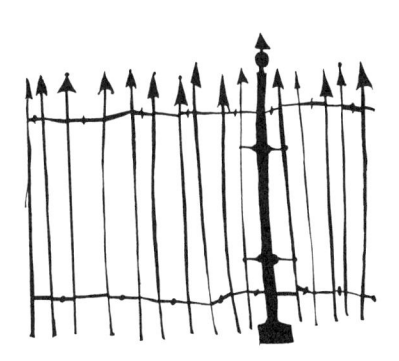

Problem X The Dilemma: Giving Form to Doubt and Fear

Describe a dilemma, that is, a concrete problem you have faced in which no solution that seems to offer itself satisfies you. Thus you are left with just the burden of the problem itself.

The "Rat in the Storm" sketch is one example of how such a paper can reveal character, feeling, mood. Notice how we come to care about the rat, not as pest or rodent, but not sentimentally either. Rat remains rat. The paper's built up well, the scene set with relevance and authority. It is not a mere thought paper: things and actions carry the mood and meaning.

In "Worse than Death," again, the particulars — narrative sequence and physical facts — keep this tense account away from mere melodrama. Seeing comes to mean more than something literal. Doubt becomes a condition of living.

In "Taste of Fear" use of direct quotes accomplishes a freedom from direct statements. This instinctive device releases drama and immediacy, reveals the essence of fear, which is uncertainty.

Rat in the Storm

I have had many personal dilemmas, but one incident last summer seems to sum up in somewhat of a symbolic fashion one of the ways I have goofed.

I was sitting in my car on the leeward side of the parking lot of the town pier in Wellfleet, Cape Cod, keeping an eye on my uncle's cabin cruiser during the most difficult hours of the peak of the last hurricane that came up the coast in early September. The sky was very dark, although it was only five o'clock or so. The wind was howling around the windows of the car and huge sheets of salt spray were sailing across the parking lot saturating everything in the way. Before the wind had reached its now roaring fury, I had doubled all the ropes fore and aft that secured the boat in its berth. The only problems could be if the slip rings on the guide posts would become caught as the boat rose past the pilings then the tide came in, and if the extra height of the tide would raise the floating dock above the limits of the slip-rings. Anyway, there I was riding out the storm in the relative comfort of my car, when my eye was caught by a small object rolling across the parking lot to the left of me. It stopped rolling some ten feet from the car. I then recognized it as a rat, very wet and frothing at the mouth. Its glassy eyes looked up at the sky as it lay on its side pawing at the air with a front foot as if it was scratching at an invisible barrier.

Several things went through my mind. Where did the poor fellow come from? There was nothing by the roaring ocean in the direction he had come from. How long had he been fighting for his life against the overwhelming odds of the wind and the sea? I could tell that he was exhausted, for at intervals he would drop his head and lie still, then commence his agonizing pawing of the air around him as he lay in a puddle of water on the pavement.

My first impulse was to save him. I could wrap him in the old towel I had with me and set him free when the storm had passed. I delayed my actions a moment as other thoughts went through my mind and then it was too late. He was rolling again. There was hope that the guard rail post lay in his path. No, he just missed it and over the embankment he went. I got out of the car with a length of rope in my hand. As I braced myself against the railing, the wind ripped at my raincoat and the saltspray felt like pellets on my back. I could see the little fellow on a small ledge halfway down to the water. He started to swim and was groping on the slippery rocks of the embankment when the swell of the sea dragged him under. He surfaced and began swimming again, his nose just above the water. But he was swimming in the wrong direction in a wide arc toward the floating dock. On the way the swell rolled him over. He was now upside down. His back arched, his head pointed straight down, his feet straight up, paddling like mad, just barely breaking the surface of the water. A few more moments of agony and he gave up and died. Floating head down, the body was carried away by the current. I turned and staggered back to my car hating myself for that moment of hesitation.

Worse than Death

One of my greatest fears is not of death, like most people, but of blindness. I've accepted my mortality, but I must die with my sight.

Two years ago, I developed severe headaches. Most doctors diagnosed this as tension, nerves. And one morning, after a worse night than usual, I woke up blind. While lying in bed, I could hear my mother doing laundry, getting my father up for work. I was awake, but just lay there for a few more minutes with my eyes shut, putting off a morning shower. Realizing it was late, I rolled out of bed, opened my eyes, and saw blackness. On the edge of panic, I called my mother. No response. Again. This time she came and I calmly explained my situation. Of course, she didn't believe me, (another ploy to get out of school?) and didn't realize I was not joking until I started fumbling around my own bedroom.

Needless to say, I never got that morning shower nor did I ever get to school. The next few days involved endless trips to the hospital, myriads of tests, and countless encounters with neurologists and surgeons. If I told my story once, it must have been twenty-five times. The problem was diagnosed as spinal fluid leaking into the brain fluid. This could affect different people in different areas of the brain. For instance, I lost my sight whereas someone else may lose their memory or hearing. I was told this could be corrected by brain surgery. A patch of skin could be placed over the leak, preventing any more fluid from seeping into the brain. If the operation was successful, the leaking would stop, but no one knew if the liquid would remain in the brain, causing permanent blindness, or if the fluid would dissipate and sight would return, whether completely or in part.

I was prepared for surgery by fasting and having my head shaved. Although that sounds trivial in light of the situation, it was one of the most traumatic experiences throughout the ordeal. I had gone into this with waist-length hair, cutting it in half for tests, then losing it completely for surgery. Before surgery time, my family visited me constantly and was a great source of strength. Before being wheeled to the operating room, my mother held me and pointed out the fact that I might not live through the operation, or might never have my sight again. As a developing artist and musician, this would be devastating. As I was wheeled away, we all cried and said goodbyes. Yet I told my mother I'd see her in a few hours. Literally and figuratively.

The operation was successful in that the hole was patched, I lived but I could not see. It was not until two weeks later that moving forms were visible, though in black and white. Things slowly and painfully returned to normal. The eyes still blur and the hair is still short. But the most amazing thing is that I can see the word I'm writing and I know what color is again.

Our family has been through a lot of emotional, physical and financial stress over these past couple years. But a fate worse than death would be to not know that strength or gift of vision.

Sight can never be appreciated to the fullest until lost for a period of an hour, a day, a week, or months. It has enriched me, embittered me, and still haunts me with pain and ailment. But to be without it, for an artist, is death-like.

Taste of Fear

I had my first taste of fear when I was a freshman in high school. On the first day all of the bullies made their hits. I was one. The guy's name was Carl Johnson. Tall, dark skinned, an earring in his ear and a mean, crazy glare in his eye. His first words to me were "Gimme a dime," and being a short, fat, baldheaded "freshie," I gave it to him. To the police it is called embezzlement, to me it is called being "messed on." Being messed on was a part of my life in my freshman and sophomore years. There's just something about it. You always know it's going to happen before it does. You get that queasy feeling in your stomach, that uneasiness called fear. I'm not going to go into all of the times that I was messed on, but one in particular I like because I came out on top.

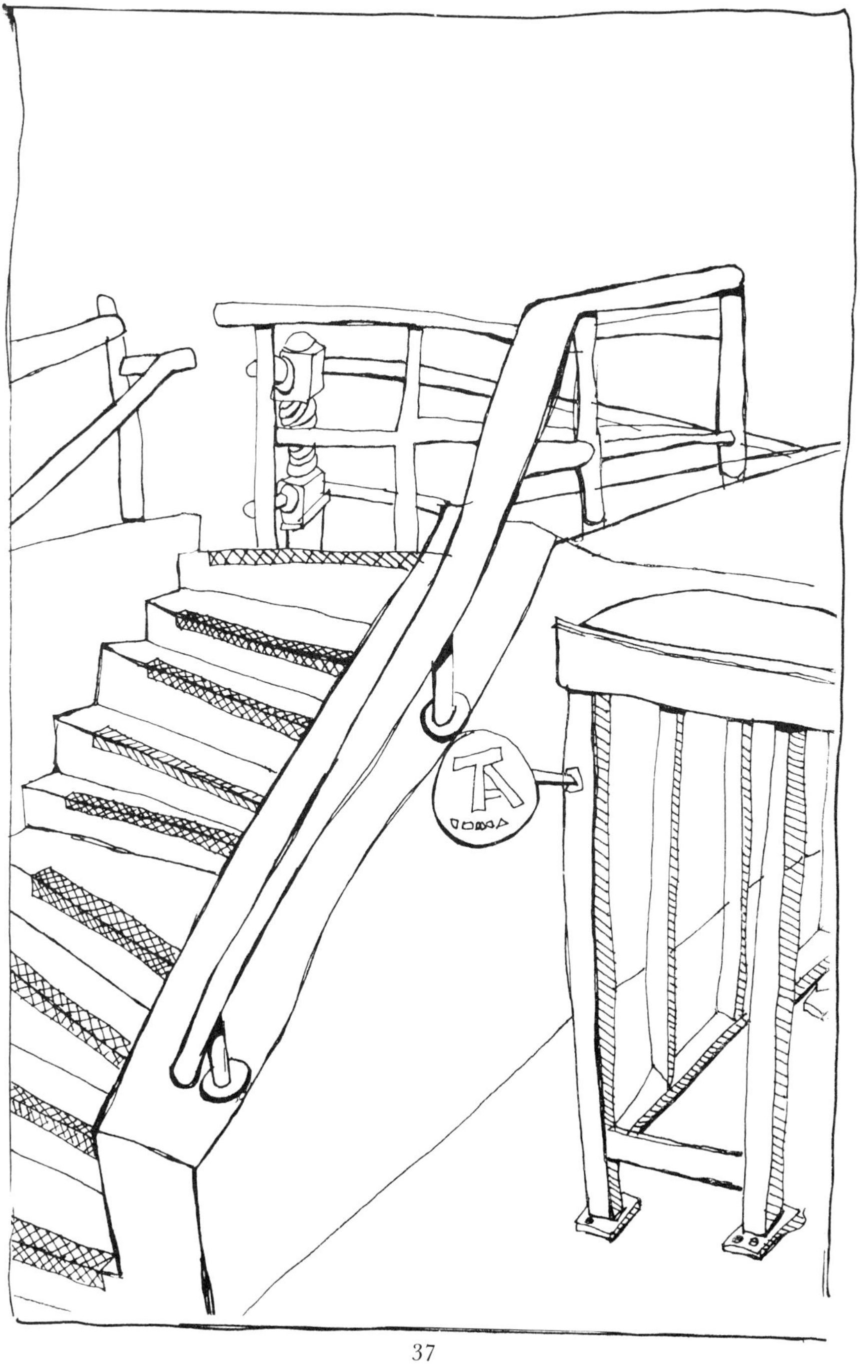

I was standing on the corner of 87th and Halsted waiting to catch my last bus home from work. I had in my right side pocket a bus transfer and a dollar bill, in my left $50. I was alone with a street light, a traffic light, and a closed news stand. Three black figures appeared from under the viaduct. The tall, thin one in the center was swinging a dog's choke chain. I knew I was going to be messed on that night. It took them about two minutes to reach the corner where I was standing. I knew I would probably end up in a fight because then I was a senior in high school and it had to be a cold day in Hell before I would let a black dude take my money, so I decided to be very arrogant about the whole thing. I didn't turn around when they walked behind me. I just acted like they were waiting for the bus too when I heard, "This is it," in a demanding tone.

"This is what?" I replied and turned around to see three black dudes pointing their pockets at me as if I'm supposed to believe they have guns in them. Now I am a black dude and I know that black dudes like to show their guns. Right away I knew that they are nothing but rookie thugs. The next line was, "You got any money, motha?"

"Naw, man, I ain't got shii."

"Yea, you want me to search you?"

"Naw, man."

"Well if you ain't got no money, how you gittin' on the bus then?"

"With a transfer, you ever heard of one of those?" I said, pulling what I thought was a transfer out of my pocket but pulling out the dollar instead.

"Gimme. Gimme that. Thought you didn't have no money," he said, snatching the dollar from my hand.

"Man, you gonna take all I got."

"You wanna git shot?" he said and walked away yelling "D" (Disciples), which was a gang cry.

After they walked away I wanted that bus to come right away, so I could wave those five tens out of the window with a smile on my face as I rode past them. But the 87th Street buses have always run slow.

Problem XI The Sketch Pad

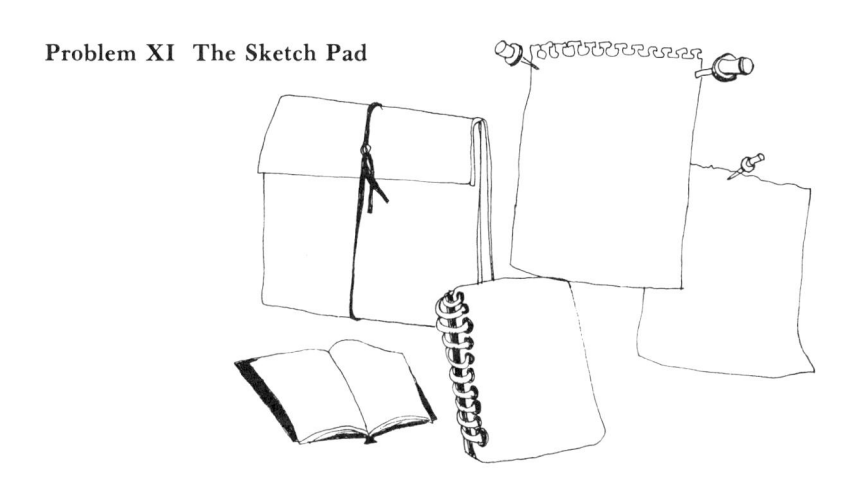

Keep a journal, a portfolio of sketches, drawings in words. For this project, write an essay every day or so, on any subject suggested by chance encounter. But keep in mind: you are not maintaining a private diary, you are not merely listing your thoughts or mentioning your moods of cheer or gloom. You are building perception from observation, thought from things. Ideas must be placed somewhere, you must put yourself somewhere to feel what you feel. Be there, but don't get in the way of your experience, don't blot it out. Rather than the abstract reference, prefer the word that weights a thing and shows itself.

This kind of personal essay is really a strong, skeptical self-statement that began with the chats of Socrates and was established by the Renaissance journal-keeper Michel de Montaigne who went up to his little study in his great chateau, away from busyness, and looked at everything with a clear eye and pen.

This is an excerpt from the introduction to his Journal:

Reader, thou hast here an honest book. I have had no consideration at all either to thy service or to my glory. My powers are not capable of any such design...In these Essays I take hold of all occasions where, though it happen to be a subject I do not very well understand, I try, however, sounding it at a distance; and finding it too deep for my stature, I keep me on the shore. And this knowledge that a man can proceed no forther is one effect of its virtue, yea, one of those of which it is most proud. One while in an idle and frivolous subject, I try to find out matter whereof to compose a body, and then to prop and support it...I leave the choice of my arguments to fortune, and take that she first presents to me; they are all alike to me. I never design to go through any of them; for I never see all of anything; neither do they who so largely promise to show it to others. Of a hundred members and faces that everything has, I take one, one while to look it over only, another while to ripple up the skin, and sometimes to pinch it to the bones. I give a stab, not so wide but as deep as I can, and am for the most part tempted to take it in hand by some new light I discover in it.

Thus, variety, shrewdness of spirit and grace of wit should mark your collection. Try out anything, don't get rutted or bogged but keep going. The experiences must be yours, but don't just live in your brain: look at the world's scenes, listen to its sounds, smell and feel it, develop that fresh dramatic sense which is a major function of the imagination. Once more, don't judge big events, don't judge at all but watch and care. Focus on one small article or piece of your day, don't hustle through everything at once. We work not from preconceived ideas but from experience; creatively, but not from unexamined fashion or bias. Revelations needn't be grand, and they're sometimes best when they're minimal.

In "Three Veiled Nuns" the start, an instant encounter in a specific place, invites us into the expansion, and reassures us of the writer's presence, involvement and perspective. The conclusion holds surprise and irony, not just an overstated "message."

With "Cold," the comparison of home to a nest of pines is a lived, not a thought-up, analogy. Notice the restrained personification of Nanny, and in "Chickens" note the earthy delight in the textures of farm routine. Yet these writers deal beyond and through cold, goat or chicken with the self as well. This combining of the observed and the felt contributes to the concept of a journal of essay sketches.

Cold

Heavily clothed, I'm walking slowly through the wet woods, which are also covered heavily with snow. Tiny snow flakes flow down at me like bullets from heaven, stinging my face until I can't feel it any more.

I go on and on, as millions of wet snow flakes crash into my clothing with a thump. Then each one disappears into my clothing. I soon become a human sponge soaking in as much as possible. My body begins itching, and my clothes get very heavy. I stomp on and on, as shiny wet twigs and branches slap my face with a sharp sting. I can now see my home, sitting in a nest of pines, like a pheasant on her eggs. She sits there with all the warmth her body can hold, just waiting for me. My fingers and toes are in desperate need for this warmth. I feel like a lost chick who has finally found his mother. I run as fast as my wet clothing will allow.

The house grows and grows, I now see gray smoke dancing around the chimney as if it didn't want to leave. Cold, and in pain from the cold, I open the door of my home with a smile of relief on my face.

Nanny

It's that time of the day when Nanny the goat is crying for attention. She can be heard by everyone on the farm, and we then know what time it is. She's always on time, no matter what, and that's the truth.

Today I'm the guy who has to take care of that creature. So I fetch the milk pail, and go out to the goat shed. When she hears me coming, she cries all the louder, until I open the door with a smile. She trots around and acts foolish. Her legs are moving very quickly as her ears slap back and forth, as if they are saying, "Good Day."

I open her grain barrel and she licks her chops eagerly when she sees the sweet grain of molasses and oats. She shakes her horns and jumps up and down, like a playful child. I give her her grain and she eats it with a thousand little nibbles. I then begin to milk her. Her bag is soft and warm to my cold winter-bitten hands. Squeeze, squirt, squeeze, squirt...for a thousand times. Well, I'm finished! The pail is full of warm foamy milk, steaming in the night air. I'm now leaving the shed, and I'm glad to be alive.

Three Veiled Nuns

Three veiled nuns today like three matched rocks in the corner of the museum lobby. Nuns in general are an oddly matched and mismatched group. A single nun is always a lonely black shadow in a crowd or a mysterious lone darkness dragging along the sidewalk. But in groups, they belong publicly so much more comfortably, like a dozen eggs. Or like three matching eggs in a museum corner.

My child's mind took flight on nun images. The metaphor changed with the order: austerely black and white veiled sisters of Notre Dame were salt and pepper shakers which didn't move, just stood there, coldly unresponsive. (This perhaps unfair to les Soeurs — my years with them were few at a tender age.) Black bonnetted Sisters of Charity weren't nuns — just old ladies with prim skirts, big shoes, and no faces. Whitely coroneted Daughters of Charity always a band of angels flurrying on snowy wings. In the wind, holding their skirts and shawls and hats, they were a bunch of crumpled paper being blown. But a single angry one was terribly like a bat descending.

It was with the Daughters of the Charity that I became most familiar. They were my teachers for most of grade school, and I came to know their species in detail from the hours of daydreamed minutes spent noting their peculiarities. Their habits offered most opportunity for speculation, perhaps because they so neuterized the wearers. Underwear was a big concern — I noticed that beneath their billowing blue sleeves were close-fitting white ones, and I wondered if this white layer existed all over or just on the arms, and if it was the equivalent of a slip. The sisters wore a starched, white bib that made their chests board-like. I would peer underneath the bib from the side, searching for a telltale bulge. But it always rather disappointed me when I did discover evidences of womanhood — most particularly the shaved napes of their necks, visible in back just beneath the coronet. It was terribly disturbing, too, to imagine them without their coronets, all clean-shaven. Most mystifying of all was that the whole garment was held together by straight pins — the coronets, white under-sleeves, everything. A great risk, I thought, especially considering that many of the sisters were very fat.

An oddly matched and mis-matched group. In all my experiences with nuns, it is hard to remember any that should have been in a convent. My third grade teacher was a freckled tomboy who told me of her stockings falling down once. Fourth grade was a huge mother hen: from behind, she spread incredibly far. Her hips bumped the desks on either side when she walked up the aisle, and the tiny pleats of her skirt swung with great vigor. She was always pulling me (her pet) into her unsuccessfully flat bosom, and clucking, or threatening to box the boys' ears. Fifth and sixth grade teachers were both old, neurotic spinsters who venged their bitterness by rapping boys' knuckles and heads with yardsticks, shaking erasers at talking girls and throwing songbooks in fits of rage. I distinctly remember having an angry admonition by my sixth grade teacher accompanied by her galoshes shaking in my face.

I remember one nun who did seem perfect. She really was an angel: appropriately pure white skin and sparkling blue eyes. She was the only one who was beautiful without makeup, and was always good and kind and gentle and soft-spoken. And she didn't have an ordinary Sister Mary Catherine name — it was Etienne. A true angel. About two years ago, Sister Etienne fell in love and soon thereafter was committed to a mental hospital. She is said to be even more beautiful with her red hair grown out.

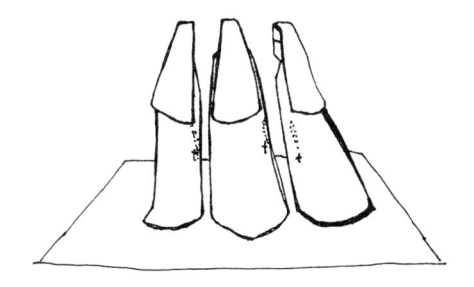

Chickens

I open the old strapped hinged door of the chicken coop, with a squeak louder than the cry of a blue jay perched somewhere in the misty woods. Immediately a strong smell of chickens and a hint of goat fill my nose and lungs. For sure I've stuck my nose into an ammonia bottle! It stings my nose and makes my lungs reject the bad air with a gasping cough.

After the rush of old air runs out the door and the new runs in, I run in with it and shut the door behind me. I could hear hundreds of feet stomping on the old sagging floor, which was packed with the animals' wastes. A hundred starving little birds run to my feet and beg with their eyes for a new batch of mash. Looking down upon them, I for once feel like a ruler of a nation, a king. And the birds are my subjects, begging for my mercy. Their heads bob back and forth with a nervous action that makes them almost impossible to watch. I open the fat grain barrel and scoop up a large scoop of mash. While filling the feeder, all I can see is bobbing heads of hungry chickens.

Problem XII A Kind of Exam: The Final Project

Choose one of the following topics and compose a carefully patterned paper of real substance to show your understanding of the principles of composition we have established.

We have emphasized the notion that an argument or an expository concept must be supported by the evidence of the senses, that is, lived experience. Render your experience concretely.

My Past and My Parents' Past

My Street or My Neighborhood

Our Photo Album

Portrait of Someone I Used to Like, But Don't Now

Skeleton in the Family Closet

The State of the Union and the State of My Soul

An Idea I have Rejected

Moments Spent Alone

We measure, remember, not mere correctness, but a concept of writing.

Metaphors hold this musing together. Aloneness turns into not trite loneliness but a condition of being perceptive, of being an artist, of keeping a self.

Moments Spent Alone

When I was little, my parents owned a farm in northern Ohio. The barn-red house and the barn-red barn had a field in back which my father sometimes tried to farm with a one-man plow, an iron contraption with long wheel-barrow handles, a wheel, and the plow blade. Mostly, the field just grew wild flowers which became, in the green harsh shine of summer, taller than I was.

I used to wander in this field along one side. There was a forest there with apple trees fringing it. They produced chubby, knotty apples which usually fell into a thickly grass-lined ditch lying between them and the field. The sky was always blue; the grass was always deep. In the ditch the sky grew over my head, and the grass swooped up to catch me in a soft, green-smelling boat. I would go there with a doll I didn't play with or a book I couldn't read. Usually my father would come and take me home after I had been gone an hour.

There was a lake in front of the Michigan house. The grass ran down until it was nipped off by the beach, and the beach until it was drowned by the water. I went there to swim in the summer and to look, often, the rest of the year.

Turning around and walking straight back by the brick walk past the house you would find, among two other buildings, the old greenhouse. Some of the glass was broken, the rest frosted and dirty. When you went in and closed the fragile, white painted door the air closed too. It became green and heavy-dirt smelling. I would go there and squat down under a limping tray-laden table. The noise outside was far away. The noise inside was still, too. By myself with my eyes shut, it was like being underwater.

After I had sat there long enough, until the air seemed too much like inside a bottle, I'd go outside and pull rhubarb with a neighbor kid, and we'd sit and squirt the juice at each other.

Of course, there was the rented house that had been a fraternity house. I was much alone there since I had the whole third floor to myself. I'd pretend I was Peter Pan and jump off my bed. On the fourth of July, I could watch fireworks out my window. I just lived up there, but on Christmas Eve, I came down and slept in my sister's room.

That was the year I got chicken-pox and broke my collar bone at the same time. I couldn't seem to make friends with other kids until my arm was back outside my clothing.

I made a diamond kite once, bigger than I was. I made it out of newspaper and balsa strips, and I took it to the school playground one day when no one was there. The string broke, and I lost my kite.

Near my home was an old golf course which the state had bought and divided in half. On one half was built a school for the deaf, and on the other a school for the blind. I'd go there sometimes with the dog, ducking under the chain-link fence. We'd go into the woods and follow the stream. The bed was wide and full of flat rocks. We had no trouble moving from side to side or climbing up the shale-sliding bank. It was dark in there with only occasional splotches of sun for the stream to splash through. The bank was often mossy and I would climb up on it and lie in the cool. Hours are short in such places. The dog would come running to nudge me, and we'd go home an involved back-sliding way for supper.

This paper seems to indicate I am only alone in places — but that is not true. I am able to spend moments alone with myself even when I'm with people. Everyone does it, I'm sure, in one form or another. Most use daydreaming.

My great dream used to be that I was going to become an archaeologist and go to Peru. I imagined myself bounding about the Andes deciphering their mysterious Inca rope system. Now my dreams are more schemes — I want to canoe down the Ohio River and on down the Mississippi. This kind of thinking is a way of living in myself. I may never do it, but I have considered it.

To be alone, you have to be still, and if you are still, far-away things intrude upon your consciousness.

Perhaps the best moments spent alone are those spent with other people.

In an amusement park.

Or a church.

Or writing an exam in a crowded hall.

AFTERWORD

Here are some comments made last day in class by freshmen. I ask them to describe the course, not to judge it — no outright statements of praise or blame, but simply objective accounts of the experience of the semester. Note how they put in the **things**, the wall, the sounds and smells of their experience: that's my victory.

These are some impressions:

The first day we had English we were asked to choose an object from the desk and write about it. There was no introduction other than the weight and feeling of our own particular object and a piece of blank paper in front of us. Pieces of broken sea glass, a thick-rimmed lime green parrot mug — we were confronted with an object and an invitation to recreate it through our own senses of touch, smell, sight and sound. Most of us missed in our first chance, but in a series of short papers we were again left to try and bring to life the integrity of the object or, later, person. For me this was a completely new approach or way of writing and of thinking. It was in a way a reversal of what I had been taught. That a piece of writing should become an entity in the same way a drawing does suddenly seemed to be a perfectly logical and obvious idea.

◊ ◊   ◊ ◊ ◊   ◊ ◊   ◊ ◊ ◊ ◊

Talking fast, anxious to have us understand his points and criticism, his speech is slowed with "ums" frequently while he searches for the right strong words. Words that sound their meaning. Very hurried, trying to put forth as many points in the hour as possible. The hands are busy, squeezing, clutching, making fists, giving further strength to his words. Grabbing the chalk with his fingers. Boldly printing with mixed lower case and capitals, trying to make us understand.

English this year was a change from the brightly lit plaster palace of three-dimensional design or the ink-and-paint-stained studios of two-dimensional design courses. Here words were used to form a design with volume, form, and shape, instead of physical materials. I wondered at the use of words and realized the difficulty of using them properly. What is a sentence but a collection of images that relate, as painting is a composition of images to form one thing.

My attitude has changed from a very subjective viewpoint to a more objective one. On the first day our teacher distributed objects to us. We were to describe shells, seaweeds, pieces of glass without naming them. After half an hour of writing we were asked to read what we had written. The only memorable piece was atrocious in its romanticism. Weeks of writing followed. Descriptions of nameless objects, characterless rooms, beautiful ugly people. I remember writing about kneaded erasers and ladybugs. We turned over, felt, and explored a piece of writing, just as we had done with the sea glass.

As far as my own writing is concerned, I have been painfully forced to realize that a piece of writing necessarily requires more than the mere exuberance of the author in order to stand. We attempted to capture rooms with real walls, pingpong balls that were round and that bounced. We worked with journal writing, an exercise in crystallizing our experiences but tempering our personalities so that they might not become overbearing. our examples were many and varied. I found too that an appreciation for literature does not come from a mere superficial look.

We started the year off right, describing objects: in my case the first was a piece of green seaglass. I got hypnotized by the rounded concavity of one side and spent most of the class stroking it with my thumb. I wrote, "The sea glass is green. One side is smooth. The other side is jagged." The teacher was not amused. "It doesn't feel like a piece of sea glass." He spoke at greater length, I am sure, but that was the essence of what he said. In due course I botched up my cotton, clouds, whatever else I tried. They didn't feel like cotton or clouds. The teacher repeated over and over, although surprisingly unexasperated, "You can't just say something, you have to show it, reveal it."

Some of the teacher's overpowering enthusiasm couldn't help but rub off. It was a good experience when it did. Among the vivid images that one might remember of the semester are the "dozen nuns like a dozen eggs," or "Roger's bad breath."

This class has been concerned with actually seeing clearly rather than thinking pompously or murkily. The idea of arriving at implied conclusions through description was presented in the earliest part of the semester as a framework, to be applied in reading, not only in writing compositions. In our writing we were to evoke the essence from plain events and objects: clay, erasers, rooms, caterpillars, rather than sentimental atmosphere. We are revealed by what we can perceive external to ourselves: the window is a mirror.

We could not have functioned amidst all this variety had it not been for the eloquent little man with the talking hands and flashing wondrous flights of beautiful speeches, modulated ideas, strings of alliterations. He moved about the front of the classroom, filling yawning gaps of silence caused by embarrassment or a state of shock. He was an alarm clock, his brisk entrance accompanied by the flicking of lights and breaking open of windows. He told us about Sartre, about Singer, about his grandmother. Sometimes we were lazy, sometimes apathetic; sometimes we appeared apathetic because it was more enjoyable to listen to him than to ourselves. We waited in breathless silence as he flipped through stacks of compositions searching for the ones he wanted to discuss with the class. Then as he read, we watched his eyebrows and listened to the tones of his voice, looking for signs that meant breakthrough or failure. The successes were gratifying, the failures disappointing. Both did us good.

Photographs by Jeanne Murray and Ted Fielding
Calligraphy by Kathryn Hardie
Thanks also to Elizabeth Schutt and the late
Professor George Sullivan
Production assisted by Beth Nelson and The Providence Eagle

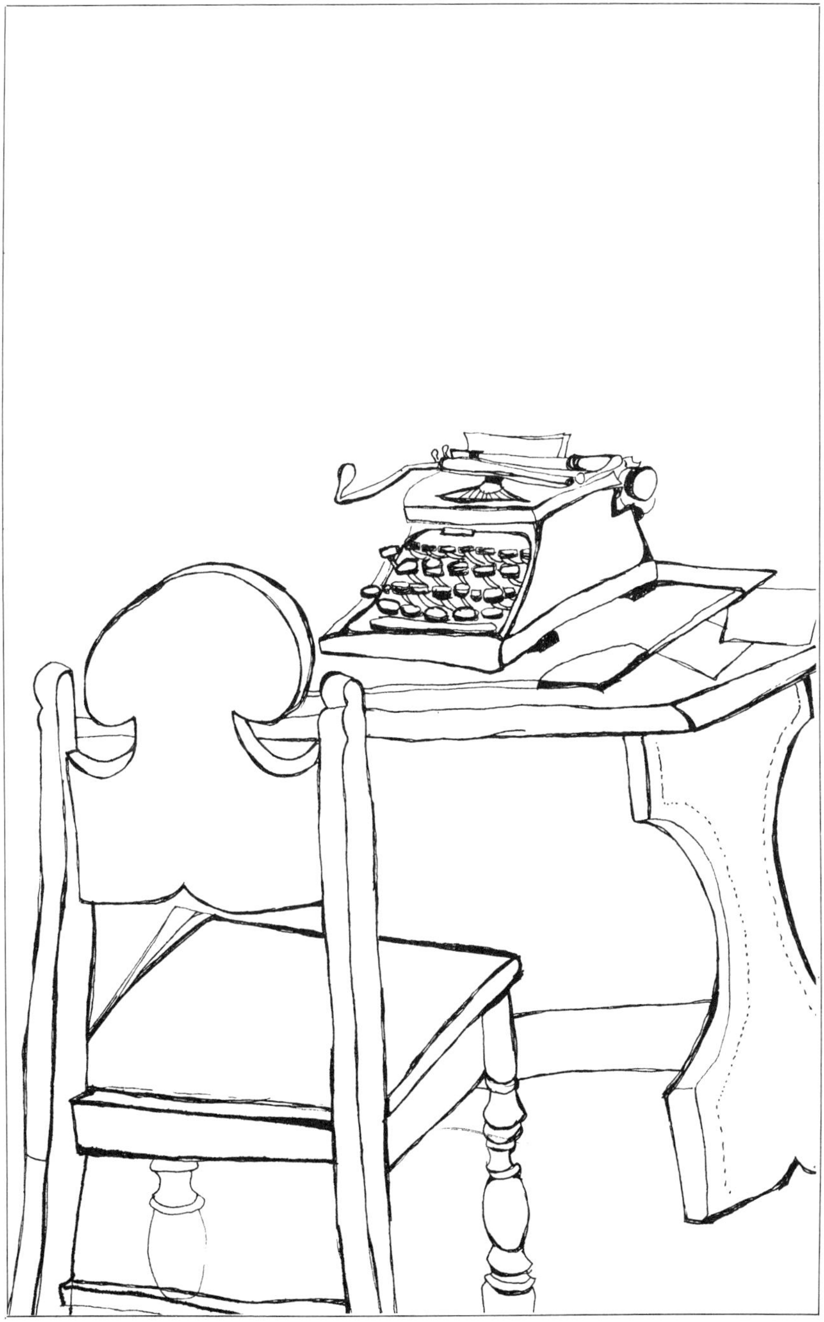